ML01593047

Disability Secrets Revealed
A Guide To Winning Your Social
Security Disability Claim

Whit Whitley

Tiana M. Hinnant

WHITLEY
LAW FIRM
1-800-863-1400

Published by PILMMA Publishing, 802 41st Avenue, South, North Myrtle Beach, SC. Contact the publisher at info@pilmma.org for more information.

Disability Secrets Revealed
A Guide To Winning Your Social Security Disability Claim

Author: Tiana M. Hinnant
Editor: Whit Whitley

ISBN:978-0-9968640-6-0

Table of Contents

About the Lawyers

Whit Whitley has practiced law since 1995 and has represented hundreds of people and their families in their Disability Claims. He has a passion for helping people get the Social Security Disability benefits they have paid for and deserve. A graduate of Norman Adrian Wiggins School of Law at Campbell University in Buies Creek, North Carolina, Whit has spent the last 21 years building a highly respected practice concentrating in Workers Compensation and Social Security Disability law.

Whit's firm, Whitley law Firm L.L.P. based in New Bern and Raleigh, North Carolina, exemplifies a passionate belief that all clients deserve to be treated with dignity and respect and have the right to receive the benefits and compensation they deserve. Mr. Whitley is Board Certified in Workers Compensation and has received the distinguished AV rating by Martindale Hubbull®. In 2015, he was selected in the Nation's Top One Percent by the National Association of Distinguished Counsel and is a member of NOSSCR (National Organization of Social Security Claimaints' Representatives). In addition to being a highly respected attorney, Mr. Whitley participates in many community service and charitable organizations.

1

Attorney **Tiana Hinnant** has practiced law since 1991. Ms. Hinnant has represented hundreds of Social Security Claimants across the Carolinas. A graduate of Wake Forest University School of Law, in Winston Salem, North Carolina, Ms. Hinnant worked in numerous areas of law through the years, including personal injury, auto negligence, catastrophic wrongful death and medical malpractice. Ms. Hinnant also worked for a number of years as an Adoption lawyer in private practice before beginning her Social Security Practice in 2008. It was not long before Ms. Hinnant discovered that representing Social Security Claimants was the most rewarding legal work she had ever done, and she continues to passionately devote her time and talent exclusively in the field of Social Security Disability. As a result, Ms. Hinnant has represented hundreds of individuals, in both North Carolina and South Carolina, helping them to obtain their much-needed and well-deserved benefits.

2

Introduction

First, we want to thank and congratulate you for taking the time and initiative to read this short, easy-to read book.

By just taking that one step... and arming yourself with all the information you need... you've already taken a huge leap towards getting the benefits you, and your family, deserve.

We can tell you from experience that most people who say they are confused and overwhelmed by their Social Security Disability claim, and are desperate for help and direction, never do anything about it. And they, and their families, suffer because of it.

Just a few of the consequences include:

- Not being able to provide for their families
- Mounting medical bills that are out of reach for the average worker
- Constant calls from bill collectors, and destruction of their credit rating
- Ongoing medical problems and no way to cover the expenses
- A lifetime of pain from injuries and disabilities that are not properly treated, or not treated at all
- Jeopardizing their rights to future benefits

That's an appalling amount of pain and suffering, along with a lot of time and money wasted. And what most people don't understand is they could have saved all that trouble and expense if they just had all the facts—and knew what questions to ask—before filing their Social Security Disability claim.

If your doctor has told you that you can no longer work— or if you've learned that with your medical impairments you

3

simply cannot sustain work—and are now facing mounting bills without any idea when or even if you can ever work again... we want you to know you are not alone.

According to the Social Security Administration (SSA), the average 20-year-old worker has a whopping 30% chance of becoming disabled before he or she reaches retirement age ... and that percentage only climbs higher as we age!

That's a shocking number of Social Security Disability claims filed ... numbering in the millions.

DID YOU KNOW: Nearly Three-Fourths of all Claims are Rejected the First Time

But the thing that truly shocks people is when they hear the number of Social Security Disability claims that are rejected every year...

The SSA's own records show that over the last 10 years, an incredible 72% of all claims are rejected the first time they are submitted... simply because they weren't filed properly, completed properly, developed properly, or the disabled person didn't know what their rights were. In fact, sometimes even deserving claims are denied at the initial level!

It sounds unbelievable that this would happen, but we've seen it ourselves, firsthand. And it contributes to what we call "Social Security Disability Disorientation," the confusion many people suffer from when trying to file for Social Security Disability Insurance.

In more than 32 years of fighting for the full Social Security Disability benefits for clients from all over North and South Carolina, we've found that a good portion of our time is spent correcting mistakes our clients have made... thinking they could do it themselves without an attorney, or thinking they had no choice but to settle for whatever the SSA offered them... before coming to us to get them the benefits they deserve under the law.

And that's why we wrote this book.

We know how incredibly confusing it can be when trying to find all the necessary information you'll need when filing a claim or trying to appeal a denial. Then juggling all that information, and have it all make sense, all while trying to figure out what is best for your unique situation... And for your family, all while suffering from an injury or disability...

That's why it's more important than ever to know how to properly file a claim, and what to look for in a Social Security Disability lawyer... Before your claim gets rejected.

In this informative, plain-language book, you'll find:

- Information on exactly what Social Security Disability Insurance is... and your rights under the law...

- The differences between an SS claim that gets rejected... and one that gets you the benefits you deserve and how to avoid the 8 common mistakes that can lead to a rejection...

- Whether or not you really need a lawyer to help file your claim...and what to look for when choosing an attorney for your disability claim...

- And you'll get answers to the 10 most often asked questions about your SS Disability claim...along with the essential checklist of important items and information you'll need to file your claim...This can mean the difference between getting the benefits you need to provide for your family while you are disabled...or getting your claim rejected, and spending months and even years fighting to get the benefits you deserve...

What we've included in this book you most likely won't find on typical lawyer websites, on government information

5

pages, or anywhere else on the Internet.

This is an honest, professional look at the information available and the rights you have under the law...
...All taken from over 32 years of protecting clients just like you... and hearing their most often asked questions, concerns and horror stories.

Having a disability that keeps you from working is a very difficult situation to go through, and the decision to hire an attorney is a big one. We trust the information you find in this book will help you make the right decision. And that it will bring you new hope and understanding... and help you finally end your Social Security Disability Disorientation... and get the benefits you deserve.

Chapter 1
What is Social Security Disability Insurance?

Before we get into all the important stuff you need to know (and watch out for) when filing your Social Security Disability claim, it's a good idea to understand exactly what Social Security Disability Insurance is, and why it's so important.

The history: In 1935, President Franklin D. Roosevelt drafted The Social Security Act as part of the New Deal. It was designed as a way to prevent what Congress saw as the dangers of life at that time: old age, poverty, unemployment and the hardships faced by widows and fatherless children.

The Social Security Act paid benefits to people who retired, those who were unemployed and paid a lump-sum benefit to families upon death.

The Act has been amended several times over the decades

since it was first enacted, to include several more categories of workers, to adjust benefits, and to establish the Supplemental Security Income and Social Security Disability Insurance programs.

Interesting trivia: The very first Social Security payment was made to Ernest Ackerman, who retired just one day after the program began. He paid in 5 cents from his paycheck and received a payout of 17 cents. (That should help should you ever find yourself a contestant on Jeopardy!)

Disability programs: According to the SSA website

"The Social Security and Supplemental Security Income disability programs are the largest of several Federal programs that provide assistance to people with disabilities. While these two programs are different in many ways, both are administered by the Social Security Administration and only individuals who have a disability and meet medical criteria may qualify for benefits under either program."

The simple explanation is this: Social Security Disability Insurance (SSDI) was created to pay you and certain members of your family monthly benefits should you become disabled and unable to work.

Supplemental Security Income (SSI) is a welfare program to assist the elderly and disabled regardless of work history and pays benefits based on financial need.

It's important to know: While Social Security Disability Insurance was created to protect American workers, that does not mean it is as simple as filing a form and getting a check mailed to your door each month.

There are many steps to filing with the SSA, lots of hoops to jump through, and any number of places you can "trip up" and have your claim rejected. As we mentioned at the beginning of this book, about 7 in 10 claims are rejected as

7

soon as they are filed, and in 2009, 64% of the filings were rejected overall.

That's why it's so important to make sure you have everything you need in order before you file. And that's why we wrote this book to help you do that so you can have a better chance at having your claim accepted.

Chapter 2
What Options Are Available to You?

If you become disabled and are no longer able to work, either short-term, long-term or ever again, there are several options available. And not all of them are equally beneficial to you.

Option 1: Don't file a Social Security claim, pay for all your expenses yourself, "suck it up" and deal with losing your wages for whatever time you are out of work, then return to work whenever you are able. That is, if you are able.

Surprisingly, many people see this as a viable option. They see it as being "independent" and not becoming a "burden to society" or draining the government's vaults. The reality is this is not true at all, and they are simply harming themselves unnecessarily. Filing a claim for SS benefits is at its core, basically an insurance claim. You paid into the system and are "insured "for benefits. You are now making a claim on that insurance.

Option 2: File your claim yourself and hope that it gets approved and the SSA makes you a fair and reasonable "favorable decision" with benefits that permit you to live and support your family. We call this the "Pay and Pray Option" because you've paid into Social Security all these years, and you pray that the nice people at the SSA recognize this and will give you everything you're entitled to, quickly and easily. Is this the way it should work, in a perfect world? Yes. Is this the way it actually happens in the real world? Sometimes, but not often enough.

Option 3: Hire an experienced attorney who has a strong focus in Social Security disability law to file or appeal for you, and fight for your rights. Notice we said "experienced attorney who focuses on Social Security Disability claims." There is a reason for this, but know that attorneys who practice a great deal of Social Security Disability law study the controlling laws very carefully, understand the ins and outs of filing claims, and have in-depth knowledge of how the SSA works... and the hoops you need to jump through to maximize your own chances of winning your case.

Chapter 3
Two Major Misconceptions about Social Security Disability

The Social Security Disability System is not fair and it is not logical. There are many rules and regulations that determine who will and who won't receive their disability benefits and working hard and paying into the SS system for many years is no guarantee that those benefits will be there for you when you really need them.

Misconception Number 1: My doctor has taken me out of work, and says that I am disabled, so I should automatically be able to receive disability benefits.

The truth is that SS will certainly consider your own doctor's opinions, but they do NOT have to agree with them. SS has their own in-house doctors, called medical examiners, who have never seen you and never treated you and who will give opinions about how sick or disabled you are and what you can and cannot do…They will say how long you should be able to sit, or stand or walk in a day, and whether you can perform simple or skilled or semi-skilled work. SS will probably send you to a doctor that they pick and they pay to examine you, called a Consultative Examiner. SS will then consider that doctor's opinion right along with your own doctor's records and opinions. Many times SS will decide you aren't disabled and give more preference to the opinions of the SS medical reviewer that works for SS or the consulting doctor that is paid by SS, even when your own treating doctor is the one who has seen you and treated you and is the one who truly knows your medical conditions and your physical or mental functioning abilities.

The path to receiving your SS benefits is not a straight shot; for most people it is a long and uphill battle. The younger you are, the steeper the hill you have to climb. SS considers anyone under 50 to be a younger individual and the rules and regulations that apply to younger individuals are stricter than for people 50 and older. And regardless of your age, and the fact that you have serious impairments like Degenerative Disc Disease or Diabetes, SS may still decide that you are capable of working.

Experienced SS attorneys know all too well just how unfair this system is. They understand the burden of proof that must be met in a case and they can prepare Medical Opinion Statements that you can take to your doctor to fill out that can help you have a stronger case and one that is more likely to result in a winning claim. These forms are designed to address the specific questions that SS will be answering when deciding your case.

If you are turned down at the Initial Stage or Reconsideration stage, as most people are, and you find that you have to go for a Hearing in front of a judge, an experienced attorney can be a great help to you. The attorney reviews all of your medical records and they know what the SS medical reviewer and the Consultative Examiners have said you can and can't do, and the attorney is prepared to make the persuasive arguments needed to deal with these opinions and to improve your chances of winning your case.

Misconception Number 2: I can't do my job anymore so SS will have to find me disabled.

As we have been discussing, the SS system simply isn't fair. It is not designed to make it easy for you to obtain your benefits and not being able to do your job anymore does not mean that SS will find you disabled. For most people, and particularly those under 50, SS looks not only at whether your impairments should keep you from doing any of your old jobs (those you performed in the last 15 years) , but also at whether you could do any other kind of work....including simple sit-down, or sedentary work, like sitting and watching a security camera, (called a "surveillance system monitor") or sitting in a quiet place putting stickers on envelopes, (called an "addresser") or watching peanuts travel down an assembly line, (called a "nut sorter")!

As incredible as it sounds, according to SS, these simple, sit-down jobs theoretically exist and many people are denied their SS benefits because SS decides that they can do this kind of work. SS uses an old and out dated book, called the Dictionary of Occupational Titles, which identifies all kinds of jobs that may have existed in America years ago, and classifies these jobs by the physical and mental exertion needed to perform the work. In our experience many of these jobs simply don't exist anymore, and if they do exist they certainly don't exist anywhere near where you live. To make matters worse, SS does NOT have to provide a ready willing and able employer in your area that is offering this

11

kind of job. All they have to do is say that this job exists, theoretically, and that they think you could do this kind of work!

Experienced SS attorneys are very familiar with the Dictionary of Occupational Titles book that SS uses, They are also familiar with the job experts, called Vocational Experts, that are usually present at SS Hearings, to give opinions to the Judges about what kind of work you use to do and what kinds of jobs you might be able to perform even with your physical or mental limitations. You might not know what to say to a Vocational Experts in a SS Hearing, but an experienced SS attorney will.

Chapter 4
A Short Outline of the Application and Appeals Process

There are 3 primary stages to a SS case. The first stage is the Initial Application; the second stage is the Request for Reconsideration; and the third stage is the Request for a SS Hearing in front of an Administrative Law Judge. Some people are approved at the Initial phase, others at the Reconsideration phase, and still others are only approved once their case is taken to an actual Hearing. As you might expect, the entire process can take months, but more often, years to complete. During that time, most people are without income and many without medical care, and feel more and more desperate as they play this frustrating waiting game.

Phase 1–The Initial Application. The Initial SS application can be prepared and submitted online at the SS website, www.ssa.gov. You can also go to your local SS office and file the application, or arrange to have the SS application done over the phone with a SS representative. In years past, when SS first stared processing online applications, these applications had to be prepared by the actual Claimant. Many times people thought they had successfully submitted the application online, only to find out months later that they had not fully submitted the claim and that it had not actually been received or processed. Fortunately, SS now allows third parties, such as a Legal Representative, to prepare and submit the online application for you. An experienced SS attorney and staff can now work with you to ensure that all the necessary information is gathered and that the Application is detailed and confirm that the Application is received and processed by SS.

In the Initial phase SS orders your records based upon the medical providers that you have listed in your application. They will not order medical records for treatment you received years ago. They will typically only order records covering the year or so prior to the date that you say you became disabled. Once the records are received they are reviewed and if necessary, you will be sent to a doctor that SS selects and that SS pays. That doctor will examine you and then provide a written report to SS that identifies your physical or mental impairments. Sometimes these doctors, called Consultative Examiners, will perform physical examinations and ask you to demonstrate what you are physically able to do in terms of sitting, standing, lifting, and showing the range of motion in your back, hips, knees, legs, etc. These Examiners may spend only a few minutes with you and barely examine you at all, or they may perform a very detailed examination.

Typically, the Initial phase of the SS case can take 2-4 months. Once SS makes their decision you will be notified in writing. You will receive a letter from SS letting you know whether they have approved or they have denied your claim.

Phase 2–the Request for Reconsideration: If your claim is denied at the Initial Phase, as most claims are, then you have 60 days in which to request an appeal, called a Request for Reconsideration.

Basically, you are asking SS to take a second look at our case. If you have undergone more medical treatment since the initial decision was made, they may order more medical records. If they have not sent you to a consultative examination at the Initial phase, they may do so now. You can expect that this phase will take between 2 and 6 months.

Unfortunately, it is also not unusual for a file to get stuck at this phase, collecting dust on someone's desk. If you have not received an answer within 6 months of requesting the Reconsideration Review, then a call should be made to SS to check on the status of your claim. Also, if you have new medical developments, such as new hospitalizations, major changes in medications or new medical providers, it is important to let SS know about these developments.

If you have a SS attorney helping you with your claim, they or their staff can contact SS to determine what is going on and encourage SS to order additional records or let them know of any new developments in your case that may make your case stronger or may lead to an approval at this phase.

Once SS makes a decision at the Reconsideration phase, you will be notified in writing. You will receive a letter from SS letting you know if you have won your disability benefits or if they are denying your claim again. Please remember that very few cases are won at the Reconsideration phase.

Phase 3: The Request for a Hearing in front of an Administrative Law Judge: If you are denied at the Reconsideration level, then you have 60 days in which to Request a Hearing in front of an Administrative Law Judge (an "ALJ"). This phase is the longest of the three.

Most people will wait 1 to 2 years from the time they request a Hearing until the time that they actually have their case heard in front of the judge. Many people become very discouraged and frustrated during this long waiting game, and rightfully so. At this point you are not working, and probably have no income at all; you are struggling to stay afloat, and keep your home and vehicle. You may be struggling to afford medical care or needed medications. Many people end up losing their homes or moving in with friends or families during this difficult time while they are waiting for their case to be scheduled for a Hearing.

There are many reasons why the Hearing phase takes so long…. As you might expect there are a tremendous number of people across the country that are applying for SS Disability. With the recent down turn in the economy many employed workers found themselves without jobs, and at an age and with physical problems that made it hard for them to find new employment.

Baby boomers are hitting their 50s and early 60s; they haven't yet reached full retirement age, and yet find themselves too sick to continue working. Judges that hear SS cases are expected to read every page of each claimant's medical files. Each medical file contains hundreds or even thousands of pages of medical records that must be read and analyzed in order for the SS Judge to understand each case and make a disability determination.

Regardless of the reasons for the backlog, the result is a long and oftentimes frustrating wait.

Dire Needs Request: If you are facing foreclosure, or eviction, or if you are receiving cut-off notices from the power company, you may be able to make what is called a Dire Needs Request. They are not always granted, and you will need a paper trail, such as a copy of the actual

15

eviction notice, or letter from the power company. There is no guarantee that the Request will be granted, but an experienced attorney will be familiar with this kind of request. If it is granted, you will not receive an automatic Hearing date, but it should move your case up further in the line, and ensure that your case is scheduled a bit earlier.

During the Hearing phase SS will no longer order your medical records. It will be your responsibility to submit records to them, or to have your SS attorney order and submit the updated medical records covering the time from the last time SS ordered them at the Reconsideration phase. If you have Medical Opinion Statements from your treating doctors, they can be submitted at this time. At some point in this phase your case will be assigned to a specific Judge and his clerk will contact you or your attorney to schedule your Hearing.

You can assume that it will take at least a year from the time you request a Hearing before SS will contact you or your attorney to schedule the Hearing.

The SS Hearing is a formal Hearing that is held at the SS Office of Disability Adjudication and Review in your area. There are Hearing offices across the country and your Hearing will be held in the Hearing office or Hearing satellite office closest to your home.

The Hearing itself lasts approximately 30 minutes to an hour, and you can expect that there will be a judge, a Hearing clerk who records the proceedings, and that there may also be a Vocational Expert (a job expert) and possibly a Medical expert. The Vocational Expert might ask you questions about the work you used to do, just to understand and better classify the work. If you have a Medical Expert in your case, they usually do not ask you any questions and do NOT examine you; they are there at the Hearing only to give testimony to the judge about what impairments they believe you have based upon their review of your medical records.

During the Hearing the Judge will probably ask you questions. If you have an attorney, the judge may turn it over to the attorney to ask you questions. The Hearing is your opportunity to tell the judge in your own words why you believe you are disabled. If you have an attorney, he or she will be able to prepare you for the Hearing, explaining the typical kinds of questions that are asked, and to give you a heads up about the kinds of questions that are loaded. They will be able to give you guidance on the best way to explain your answers.

The judge will be familiar with your case, and will typically have reviewed all of your medical records. Since they already know what is in your file, the Hearing is their opportunity to hear from you, in your own words, as to why you are no longer able to work. They will typically ask you to tell them what impairments, or medical problems you have that you feel keep you from working. They may ask you about your activities of daily living, such as whether you drive, do household chores or yard work. Sometimes they will ask you to describe your past work.

During the Hearing, and even if your judge is asking the questions, your attorney will be listening and will probably take notes and determine what follow up questions need to be asked so that you are able to fully explain your answers and so that the judge is able to see that you are no longer able to do any of the work you use to do, and are not able to do any other kind of work full-time.

You do not have to have an attorney with you at a SS Hearing, but if you do have an attorney, then they will be able to talk on your behalf, and to help you tell your personal story to the judge. They are familiar with the judges, the

17

experts, the kinds of questions that are normally asked, and the pitfalls that need to be avoided. If you have an attorney by your side at the Hearing, you are not alone, and you will have someone with you who also knows and understands your medical file and the rules and regulations that SS will be applying and can help explain why your case fits squarely within those rules and why you should be found disabled.

Most of the time the Judge will NOT make a decision at the time of the Hearing. Instead, he or she will take the matter under advisement. They will go back and read and review their notes and they will make a written decision and that written decision will be mailed to you and to your attorney.

See Figure 1 on the following page for an illustration of the SS Disability time line.

Chapter 5

The SSA's 5-Step Sequential Evaluation Process

When you file your SS claim, the Social Security Administration will put it through a 5-step evaluation process to determine if you are disabled, determine the extent of your disability, and see whether you are eligible for disability payments through the SSA.

This evaluation is made by an examiner, along with the Disability Determination Services department (DDS), including a medical team that reviews each case file.

To qualify for evaluation, first you must have worked and paid into the Social Security program for 5 of the last 10 years, and have been disabled before reaching full-retirement age (65-67). If that's the case, then you must pass each of the

The Social Security Disability Application Timeline
For Social Security Disability Application Approvals & Reconsideration Requests

INITIAL APPLICATION
Initial Application is sent to your Social Security District Office Determination Service.

0 MONTHS

FIRST DECISION
If your application is rejected, you still have two more appeals.

6 MONTHS

The average wait time after an application is sent is 6 months.

The Next Step: If your claim is approved, congratulations. If your claim is denied, we file for a "reconsideration."

8 MONTHS

Appeal Deadline
If your initial application is denied, you must submit an appeal within 60 days.

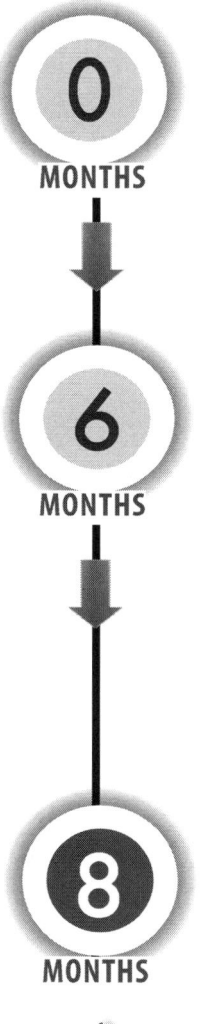

Timeline is based on national averages and actual wait may vary.

14 MONTHS

RECONSIDERATION DECISION

If you are denied, you can request a hearing with an Administrative Law Judge.

It takes an average of 6 months for a decision to be made for a reconsideration appeal.

The Next Step: If your claim is approved, Carolina Disability Lawyers will explain the payment process. If your claim is denied for a second time, continue on the timeline.

16 MONTHS

Deadline to Appeal for Hearing

You have 60 Days to submit your appeal for a hearing. Appeal to your Social Security District Office Determination Service.

The average wait time for a hearing is almost 12 months.

THIRD DECISION

52% of all South Carolina hearings are in favor of the applicant.

28 MONTHS

The Final Step: If you are denied, Carolina Disability Lawyers can help you file a new application and restart the timeline.

5 steps—and not meeting the requirements of any step along the way will get your claim rejected.

Step 1: Are You Working?

We call it "working" the SSA calls it "engaging in substantial gainful activity" or SGA. (The government loves giving things complicated titles—and this is not just a term or definition, it is more of a concept or a "legal term of art"...)

Basically, the SSA is looking to see if you worked and earned more than $1,170 per month on a sustained basis. ($1,950 if you are blind). If so, that's enough to likely get you disqualified from receiving Social Security Disability payments.

Note: The SGA amount is reviewed every year, and may change each year.

Step 2: Is Your Condition Considered Severe by the SSA?

Your condition must be "severe" enough to interfere with your ability to perform the most basic work activities required in any job. This can include: seeing, hearing, speaking, walking, sitting, reaching, responding to supervisors, etc. (By now, you may have guessed that "Severe" is also a "legal term of art" and can get complicated.)

If your disability is considered "severe" under the regulations, then they will move to Step 3.

Step 3: Is Your Disability on either of the SSA's Lists of Disabling Conditions?

The SSA has two lists of conditions it considers disabling—one list for children and one for adults. The adult list breaks conditions into fourteen high-level categories according to body system. We refer to these lists of conditions as "The Listings".

If your specific condition is not listed, then the DDS (a

State Agency that makes the medical decisions at the lower adjudication levels) will look to see if it is "equal" to one of the disabling conditions on the list.

This is really a cut and dry decision, either you meet/equal one of the conditions or not. If not, then we move to Step 4. These listing are very specific and meeting them is difficult for most people. An experienced SS lawyer will be familiar with these listings and whether you can show SS that your case meets or equals them.

Step 4: Can You Do the Same Work You've Done in the Past?

The DDS will look to see if you are able to do the same work that you have done in the past, despite your disability. If you can, they will deny your claim.

If you cannot, they will proceed to the fifth and final step...

Step 5: Are You Able to do any other Type of Work?

So you can't perform your current work... but can you perform ANY other work at all? That's what they will look at next.

The DDS will review your age, education, physical/mental condition, skills, and work experience to determine what other work, if any, you're able to perform. If they find you are able to switch jobs and be able to work, they will deny your claim.

IMPORTANT NOTE: Merely making it to Step 5 is not a guarantee that your claim will be approved. The burden of proof shifts to the SSA at Step 5, but they have many ways to meet their burden of proof, which can result in a denial of benefits. In fact, there are several pitfalls which can lead to a denial:

- Not cooperating with the Social Security Administration

22

- Failing to return paperwork
- Not showing up for Hearings
- Not submitting to a doctor's examination by a physician of their choosing
- Being under the influence of drugs or alcohol

And this is just a partial list.

Following directions and making sure you supply the SSA with everything they ask for is crucial to getting your claim accepted. Even then, nothing is truly guaranteed. However, mistakes along the process can get your claim rejected quickly, and you can read The 7 Most Common Mistakes That Can Get Your Claim Denied in the next section.

Chapter 6
The 7 Most Common Mistakes People Make

It can be a long journey to ensure your Social Security Disability Benefits claim is accepted and you get all your entitled benefits—and this journey begins before you even sit down to fill out your application.

Unfortunately, most people have no idea what they need to do to make sure they have all the proper information ready and they fail to take all the necessary steps to get their claim in order no matter what administrative level they are dealing with.

So many claims get rejected every year simply because mistakes were made along the way.

This is why we have compiled this list of the "7 Most Common Mistakes You Can Make When Claiming Your

Social Security Disability Benefits."

Read this list carefully to make sure that you know what these common pitfalls are and that you understand how you can avoid them. (Again, even if you do everything right, you may still get denied and find yourself in front of a judge. There is no way of knowing for certain in advance, but we always work with two concepts: Preparation and Education.) If you have any questions or concerns regarding your application and claims forms, always seek the help of an experienced SS lawyer.

Common Mistake 1: Delay Applying for Your Disability Benefits

The Social Security Administration states that in order for you to be considered "disabled" you must be unable to work due to health issues for a year or longer.

Many people make the mistake in thinking they must be out of work for a year before they are eligible to apply for benefits – this is not correct.

Once you stop working due to health issues and you expect you will be out of work for a year or longer, it is always best to file an initial application immediately. You don't have to wait until you have been sick a full year – you may have stopped working last week, but if your impairments are not getting better, and you aren't able to return to work, then you can file your claim right away.

The process to ensure you receive all your entitled Social Security Disability benefits begins long before you fill out your claim form.

If you are unable to work, you need your benefits as soon as possible.

The disability process could take years to complete, especially if your case is subject to reviews, Hearings and appeals. This could result in financial hardship for you and your family.

Applying for your Social Security Disability benefits as soon as you reasonably believe you are disabled is wise if you want to avoid a delay in receiving your disability benefits once you are approved. Consider also that the "look back period" or "retroactive effect" of a SSDI claim is only one year. If you wait longer than a year to apply, you may be leaving money on the table.

Common Mistake 2: Failing to Prepare for Your Claim

Preparation is your best defense when you present your Social Security Disability claim.

Be sure you obtain current medical records, follow your doctor's orders and take all prescribed medications as directed.

File Hearing requests and appeals within the specified time frame and attend all medical appointments and court dates.

Your Disability Report is one of the most important parts of your application process.

This form provides information about your disability and the Social Security Administration uses this report to determine your personal assessment of disability.

Be prepared with all of the important information you need to file your claim.

Common Mistake 3: Not Listing All of your Physical and Mental Illnesses on your Application

If you hurt your knee in a car accident, then hurt your back years later in a separate accident – don't make the mistake of thinking you can only file for benefits under "one" injury.

Social Security Disability allows you to list multiple

injuries that may show you qualify for disability benefits. Even psychiatric treatment can help you to qualify for disability benefits.

That's why it's important to list all of your injuries and disabilities when applying for benefits.

It's easy to misinterpret what the Social Security Administration is asking from you and many people provide the wrong information on their application and claims forms.

This application process may seem complicated, confusing and time consuming. Many people become overwhelmed with the process, particularly when they are already sick and in pain. That is why it is important to know that SS now allows a third party, such as an attorney to assist you in this process. They can work with you making sure that the application is filled out clearly and with all the necessary details.

Common Mistake 4: Getting an Unconvincing Statement from your Doctor

Some claims are initially denied based on the statement from your doctor.

If your doctor believes that you are disabled, but his statement does not meet the criteria required by the Social Security Administration for approval—or even worse, your doctor makes legal determinations as opposed to just providing medical opinion evidence— then it's possible your claim may be denied.

It's important that your doctor determines you are "totally disabled" according to SSA definitions and provides you with the medical records and statement to back up such a claim. Just making statements like "this patient is totally disabled" are helpful, but not really what we look for to maximize your chances of winning.

26

Lawyers who routinely handle SS cases are experienced in dealing with doctors and medical records. They know what to look for in the evidence, ways to phrase things, and can speak with your doctor and make sure that his or her statement is thorough, precise and meets the requirements necessary to help you get your disability benefits. Experienced attorneys can provide you with forms to take to your doctor that are designed to show SS that you meet the specific criteria that SS looks for to approve your claim.

Common Mistake 5: Not Getting the Medical Treatment your Doctor Recommends

In order for you to qualify for Social Security Disability benefits, you must be unable to do any substantial work due to your medical condition.

According to the Social Security Administration your medical condition must have lasted, or is expected to last, at least one year, or be expected to result in your death, in order to be defined as "totally disabled."

Again, it is important that your doctor determines you are disabled according the guidelines given by the SSA. Your doctor will need to provide you with the medical records to back up your claim.

If you don't listen to your doctor's advice and get the medical treatment recommended, you may be unable to qualify for disability benefits. Evaluations of your condition and level of disability may be based on whether or not you have followed procedures and treatments prescribed by your doctor.

You can avoid this mistake by making sure you go to all your doctor appointments and follow all instructions given, such as getting prescribed medical treatments and taking your medications. In fact, please keep a diary of your medical appointments – better, get a business card from each doctor,

27

clinic or hospital, etc. and tape it to an inexpensive calendar that you write all your doctor and therapy appointments on. This can help you remember your appointments and help make sure you tell SS or your lawyer about all your treatments.

Common Mistake 6: Working While Filing for Benefits

The Disability Determination Service (DDS) determines your qualification for disability based upon two major factors:

- Limitations due to your medical impairment
- How these limitations impact your ability to work

It's important that you know your limitations before you attempt to apply for any type of employment.

The Social Security Administration will check to see if you are working. (Remember, this is defined as "engaging in substantial gainful activity" or SGA, with gross income of approximately $1100 or more per month.)

If you are working, even if only part time, it may hurt your chances for approval. It is technically possible to work and apply for disability, and not lose your case just because you are working. However, it is a complex area of the law involving several Regulations and Rulings. Your own results are going to be very fact dependent- so, get detailed, specific legal advice about this topic. Also please do not confuse this issue with other common areas of confusion: working after you have been approved for benefits. That is another lengthy topic!

An Administrative Law Judge may determine you are able to continue working in some capacity, even if you are unable to return to your old profession, and therefore deny your application.

Common Mistake 7: Giving Up Too Soon

28

Applying for Social Security Disability benefits can be a long and daunting process. Unfortunately, many people decide to give up.

It can take months to get an initial decision. If you are denied, you need to appeal and file a Request for Reconsideration. It can sometimes take a few more months for a Reconsideration decision. The next appeal is a Request for Hearing, and there is a typical wait time for a Hearing. That wait varies by which Hearing office will have jurisdiction, and even then, is something of a moving target. In Boston, Massachusetts the wait time is 13 months; in Charlotte, North Carolina it's currently 19 months, in Tallahassee, Florida the current wait time is 20 months!

From start to finish, a case can take anywhere from a few months to a few years. Our experience is that most cases usually take approximately 1-2 years.

All that paperwork required by the Social Security Administration to apply for your disability benefits can be confusing. It's easy for you to misinterpret what the SSA is asking from you, and you can make avoidable errors on your application and claims forms.

Try to be persistent and patient. Whatever you do, don't give up.

Chapter 7

7 Secrets to increasing your chances of Winning Your SSD Claim

Secret #1–You Must Provide the Necessary Documentation Needed When You Initially Apply

One of the primary reasons applications are denied is a

lack of supporting documentation.

That's why you need to make sure that your initial application is as complete as possible. Yes, we understand the application process can be very time consuming, but not getting everything together for the SSA is one reason so many applications are initially denied.

And if your initial application is denied, the Reconsideration process may take as long as 4-6 months, sometimes longer. This translates into thousands of dollars in missed benefits and could result in financial hardship for your family.

The Social Security Administration requires that original documents be submitted with your application for benefits. You may take them to the local SSA office or mail them in with your application. The SSA will copy the documents and return the originals to you. The types of original documents required are:

- Proof of age (i.e., birth certificate) and Social Security Number (SSN)
- List of employers and the type of work you did - typically for the last 15 years
- W-2 forms for the last 10 years or tax returns, if you were self-employed
- Names, addresses and phone numbers for all doctors, hospitals, therapists, clinics, etc. that you have visited and the dates of all visits
- Complete medical records, including laboratory and test results
- Listing of all medications you are currently taking and the dosage of each
- Adult Disability Report (Form SSA-3368)

The information you provide will be reviewed by the Disability Determination Services.(DDS) department and discussed at your disability application interview.

Helpful Hint: The SSA provides free worksheets online to help you compose your thoughts and gather the necessary information needed for your application. Keep in mind that these are forms for your personal use and are not to be filed with the SSA… The regular application must still be completed.

If your family members are also applying, you will need proof of age and Social Security Numbers for each individual and a marriage certificate if your spouse is applying.

You may also want to complete and submit the Authorization to Disclose Information to the Social Security Administration (Form SSA-827) along with your application. This form grants permission to the DDS department to request additional medical records, if needed.

Secret #2–How to Get a Quicker Decision

You can help get a faster decision from the Social Security Administration on your application by following a few simple guidelines.

The timeliness and completeness of your initial application are very important. Missing information could result in a delay of processing your application and possibly a denial. Equally important are the following tips to help you get a quicker decision:

- Respond promptly to any request by the Social Security Administration or the Disability Determination Services department to provide additional information.

- Attend all Hearings on the date, the time and at the location they tell you.

31

- Keep your contact information with the SSA up to date. If you move or change phone numbers let them know immediately.

The SSA does have two initiatives in place for extreme cases that may help expedite certain types of claims. The first is referred to as "Compassionate Allowances."

This typically applies when a condition is known to be fully disabling or terminal. This includes diseases like Atrophic Lateral Sclerosis (ALS) or pancreatic cancer. (You can go online http://www.ssa.gov/compassionateallowances/conditions.htm and see the entire list of compassionate allowances. It was recently expanded.)

The second is referred to as "Quick Disability Determinations."

This refers to a computer screening model which identifies cases that are highly likely to be approved, and fast-tracks them.

As of 2010, the Quick Disability Determinations model only handled the most extreme disabling conditions. Decisions in cases using the model were typically made in around 12 days. (But understand, in our experience, this is rarely used.)

An experienced lawyer may be able to find a way to expedite your claim. This depends upon your specific situation. Please note that if you are waiting on a Hearing date, there are some limited ways to expedite a Hearing by showing "dire need," such as foreclosure/eviction, utility cut off, terminal disease, wounded warrior, and others.

Secret #3–Getting Objective Tests Performed by Qualified Medical Professionals

You cannot win your Disability case without strong medical records!

A SS caseworker or a SS Judge may like you, and they may see that you have medical conditions that limit your ability to work, but their hands are tied and they cannot approve you unless they see medical records that support what you say you can or can't do.

What you say you can or can't do is called Subjective Evidence. Even your doctor's statements about your disability status or limitations are considered Subjective Evidence. While SS wants to know this Subjective information, you cannot win a disability case on Subjective evidence alone. There must be Objective medical evidence in your file. This means test results that show clear medical impairments or conditions. Examples of Objective tests are MRI results, CT scan reports, Lab values from blood tests, Pulmonary Function Reports, EMG nerve conduction tests, X-rays, etc.

No matter how sick you say you are; No matter how sick your own doctor may say that you are: SS expects to see Objective Medical evidence in your medical records that backs this up. For example, you may say that you have chronic back pain, and that it hurts you to stand for very long, or sit for very long, or even to drive a car for very long. Your doctor may be prescribing pain medication, or muscle relaxers, or may have given you a Tens unit or a back brace or even prescribed a cane for you to use for balance and support when walking. Even with that kind of evidence, SS will look to see if there are any Objective findings in your medical records that support this. They will look to see if you have X-rays that show Degenerative Disc Disease, and whether the report says it is mild or minimal or severe. They will look to see if you have an MRI report on your back, and whether it shows foraminal narrowing, or nerve encroachment, herniation, bulging etc.

If you have Diabetes and you say that you have numbness and burning and tingling in your hands or in your feet,

33

your doctor may be prescribing Gabapentin and you may be walking with a cane. SS will look to see if you have had Nerve Conduction studies that show that you have diabetic neuropathy. Your subjective complaints of pain will not be enough. Objective medical evidence is essential for a winning case.

If you can't afford to go to the doctor, and have no health insurance and no income this burden may seem impossible. Don't give up!

An experienced SS attorney can give you lists of free or sliding scale clinics in your area where you can obtain medical care and treatment. Many times there are charity programs through local hospitals if you know where to look and who to ask. And, of course, many people find themselves at their local emergency rooms for care and treatment when they do not have a medical doctor.

Please remember that it is very important that you let your attorney or SS know where you are going for any kind of medical care or treatment so that all these records are ordered, and so that any objective tests are obtained and submitted to SS for review.

Secret #4–You Must Order and Get Your Own Medical Records for Your Hearing before a Judge

SS does not make it easy on you when you are seeking your disability benefits! When your Hearing date arrives, the judge will be looking at whatever is in your file at that time. It is very important that you submit ALL the medical records that SS does not already have. SS orders your medical records at the Initial Phase and they order them at the Reconsideration phase. But they do NOT order your medical records once you reach the Hearing phase. It is up to you or to your attorney, if you have one, to order all the medical records for all medical treatment you have received since the

34

Reconsideration stage.

You may need to pay for these medical records up front, depending on the individual medical provider. If you are working with an attorney then they will order your medical records and pay for them, and will probably seek reimbursement only after you win your disability.

The important thing to remember is that your case is won or lost, in large part, by the Medical Records, and particularly the Objective Medical findings in those records. The more records you have that show and explain your impairments and limitations, the stronger your case and the better shot you have at a win.

You will want to fax your medical records to the SS Hearing office, or you can electronically submit them if you know how to do this via computer and if you have the necessary barcode.

Secret #5–Get Your Treating Doctor and Any Specialists You've Seen to fill out a Physical Capacities Evaluation Form

Having your own treating doctor fill out a Medical Opinion Statement detailing your medical impairments and how they limit your functioning ability can be worth its weight in gold to your case!!

If you don't have the medical opinion of your own treating doctor that supports your disability claim, then SS will be relying on the medical opinions of a medical reviewer that is a paid SS employee---someone who has never seen you or talked to you, much less treated you for your condition.

SS may also look at the opinion of the Consultative Examiner, if they sent you to one. Remember, these Consultative Examiners may be private doctors, but they are paid by SS to do exams and give reports to SS. It is a rare consultative report that is actually helpful to you! If at all possible you do NOT want SS to be basing its decisions on the medical opinions of doctors who work for or are paid by SS and seldom give favorable opinions about your medical impairments or resulting limitations.

So whenever possible you want to have and submit a strong medical opinion statement from one of your own treating doctors, and preferably a specialist if you are being treated by one.

Experienced SS attorneys are very familiar with these Medical Opinion Statements. Most of the time, they have forms prepared for your treating doctor to fill out. Sometimes these forms are very specific and designed to show that you meet particular Listings within the SS rules and regulations.

Sometimes these Medical Opinion forms are designed to show what impairments you have and ask the doctor to give opinions about your functioning ability based upon their knowledge of your medical case. They will usually ask the doctor to approximate how long you can sit, stand or walk at one time, and whether you will need frequent unscheduled breaks, or whether you will likely miss 2 or 3 or more days per month due to your impairments and treatment.

An experienced SS attorney will know what kind of Medical Opinion Forms you need and they will be designed to address the very issues that they know SS will be looking at when deciding your case.

It is very important that you have medical records from that treating doctor that supports his or her opinions. Otherwise, SS will basically dismiss your doctor's opinions. That is why it is so important that you seek medical treatment regularly, tell your doctor all the problems you are experiencing every time you go, and that you follow their recommendations and take all medications as prescribed.

You want to make your case as strong as possible and it can only be strong when you have strong medical treatment records.

Secret #6–Understand That the Social Security Administration is Trying To Find Ways To Deny Your Claim and Not Accept Your Claim

Simply stated, SS is NOT your friend! They are NOT looking for ways to approve your claim: they are typically looking for ways to turn you down. When you talk to a SS representative and they are nice or polite, you may assume that they like you and that they are going to approve your claim. For most people that is not the case. Most people are turned down at the Initial or the Reconsideration stage, regardless of how nice the Examiner or Case reviewer seemed over the phone when they called to speak with you about your case.

Whenever you talk to a SS representative, or a doctor they send you to, or even a Judge at a SS Hearing, it is important to remember that they will NOT assume any limitation that you do not tell them. If they ask you if you drive, and prepare your meals, and do the shopping and cleaning and cooking in your home, what they are really trying to decide is if by being able to do all that stuff, you can probably handle some simple sit-down work…. You might think that telling them all the things you do will show that you are a strong person, pushing through your pain, and just trying to deal with your illness as best you can. You might think that you will seem more deserving of your benefits as a result of these things.

Unfortunately, and for most people, their words are used against them in a SS case! SS will NOT assume any limitations that you do not tell them. You must make it very clear that you have limitations in your cooking and cleaning…or that you are NOT able to drive every day, that

37

your driving is limited to only the occasional "good" day and for short distances only, because of pain, side effects of medications, etc.

Use every question that SS asks you as an opportunity to discuss what you can't do, or your limitations, rather than what you can do. Most people who are disabled have good and bad days. Some days they are struggling with unbearable pain all day and then occasionally they have a good day, where they might attempt to do some grocery shopping, or light cleaning, etc. For most people their bad days far outweigh their good days. If that wasn't the case, they would not even be applying for disability....

You should answer all the questions SS asks you or the Consultative examiner asks you based upon what your life is really like on an average real day and not on the occasional good day, and NEVER answer just "yes" to any question without explaining your limitations or difficulties.

Secret #7–Be Complete When Talking to Your Own Treating Doctor!!

Many people completely derail their SS case by the simple things they say or don't say to their own treating doctors. When you go in to see your doctor, particularly one who is familiar with your case, you probably don't feel the need to tell them all the things that are wrong with you, and all the regular problems that you experience on a daily basis. If they are treating you for arthritis and you have pain in your legs, feet or knees, you may not tell the doctor about it. You may well assume that he knows this and then just tell him about any new pain. That seems reasonable, of course, but can be awful for your SS case. That doctor might well write down, no new complaints, or "doing fine" or "feeling good today"... When in fact you may be in a great deal of pain, and you just aren't talking about it, either because you feel he already

38

knows this, or because you don't want to be a whiner.

However, because SS is typically looking for ways to turn you down, they will jump on that kind of language in a medical record and use it to say that you had no limitations at that time, or that your condition was improving.

What you need to remember is that your case will rise or fall based in large part by what your medical records say or don't say. So tell your doctors everything that is hurting you every single time you go to the doctor.

Chapter 8

8 Things That Will Get You Denied Automatically

It's natural to think about the reasons why you should be granted Social Security Disability benefits, but consider the reasons why your claim might be denied.

It is important to understand that the Social Security Administration will automatically deny claims in certain situations. Below are 8 things that could result in your claim being denied.

1. Your application is incomplete or lacks supporting documentation.

2. You are able to perform your usual work.

3. You are able to perform another type of work.

4. You have an insufficient number of work credits.

5. Your impairment is not considered severe.

6. Your disability is not expected to last at least 12 months or be terminal.

7. Your impairment is primarily due to drug or alcohol

abuse, or that abuse is material to what disables you.

8. You fail to cooperate with the SSA or follow prescribed medical treatment (without good reason).

The Social Security Administration will also deny your claim if you have returned to Substantial Gainful Activity (SGA) before your case is decided, and you have been off work less than 12 months.

Sometimes if you return to SGA level work after you have been out of work for 12 months, you can try to be paid by the SSA for the time you were off. We call this a "closed period" of disability, and an experienced SS lawyer can sometimes help clients obtain these limited benefits.

Take time to review the SSA's guidelines regarding disability to ensure you meet these guidelines before you file your application.

If you have questions about what it takes to qualify for disability, this is a good time to seek out an experienced lawyer. Getting sound advice on the front end can make a world of difference, and save you trouble down the road.

Chapter 9

What to Do If You Are Denied: 4 Levels of Appeals

For most people, the initial application process can be overwhelming.

Since you are not experienced in dealing with the Social Security Administration on a regular basis, it is likely that your initial application for Social Security Disability benefits may be denied. And like we've mentioned in other parts of this book, nearly 70% of applications are denied.

The decision makers at lower levels in the SSA only have your file to review. That's all. They rarely look beyond your medical evidence, which is why it's so important to maintain good records.

But don't give up! If you are denied, you can appeal, and your chances of success improve significantly. If your initial disability application is denied, there are 4 Levels of Appeals that you may go through.

Appeal Level 1: File an Appeal for Reconsideration

If your initial claim is denied, you can file an appeal for Reconsideration by the state Disability Determination Services department.

This initial appeal may be submitted online by completing the Appeal Request Internet Form and the Appeal Disability Report (Forms SSA-561 and SSA-3441). You may also call or visit your local SSA office and tell them you wish to appeal a disability ruling.

When you submit a formal Request for Reconsideration (Form SSA-561-U2), your claim will be assigned to a different examiner and medical team for review. So any additional medical information to support your claim should be provided in your Appeal Disability Report. That's because reconsiderations are a completely new review of your claim by someone who did not take part in the first decision.

IMPORTANT: It is important that you submit your appeal no later than 60 days after the date of denial of your initial claim (plus 5 days grace for mailing, but it is best to not even get close to the 65 day limit). If you were receiving SSI or SSDI benefits and the SSA terminated those benefits, you have only 10 days to appeal.

TIP: keep the envelope the denial came in, you may need the postmark to show WHEN you got the denial

41

On average over the last 10 years, only 3% of denials were overturned at the reconsideration level.

Appeal Level 2: Request a Disability Hearing

If your case is denied again (for example, you get a Reconsideration denial), you may appeal this denial and request a Disability Hearing before an Administrative Law Judge (ALJ).

Note: some states have eliminated the Level 1 reconsideration process altogether, and take appeals straight to a Disability Hearing.

Over half of Social Security disability claimants who appeal to the administrative Hearing level are ultimately awarded disability benefits.

Why are your chances so much better at a Hearing?

The Social Security Disability Hearing gives you a chance to meet with an Administrative Law Judge (ALJ) in person. (And don't think of this as a bad thing. This is really the face-to-face meeting you've been waiting for.) The judge will evaluate your entire case, listen to your testimony, make credibility assessments, and determine whether you are disabled under the terms of the Social Security Act.

Appeal Level 3: Request A Review By An Appeals Council

If an Administrative Law Judge denies your case, you may request a review by the SSA's Appeals Council.

Understand that the Appeals Council may deny your request if it believes your Hearing decision was correct.

If the Appeals Council decides to review your case, it will either decide your case itself or return it to an Administrative Law Judge for further review, and you will receive notification along with a copy of the Appeals' Council Order.

If the Appeals Council denies your request for review, you

will receive a letter explaining why you were denied.

Appeal Level 4: Federal Court Hearing

If the Appeals Council denies your request for review, you may file a lawsuit against the Federal Government in a Federal District Court.

The first thing you will need to do if your case goes before a federal court is to hire an experienced and qualified lawyer. Only a licensed attorney can represent you in court.

The majority of your federal court Hearing is conducted in writing with written briefs being submitted by both parties –you (the Plaintiff) and the Social Security Administration (the Defendant).

In some cases, the Court may request an oral argument of your case.

Should this happen, your lawyer and the lawyer who represents the Social Security Administration will argue your case before the Federal Judge behind closed doors.

Chapter 10

7 Crucial Questions You Should Ask Before Hiring Your Disability Lawyer

If you decide to hire a lawyer to handle your disability claim, you'll want to meet or talk with several lawyers before you make your final decision on which one to hire.

Choosing the right lawyer for you requires some research, some diligence and asking the right questions.

You need to determine basics such as his or her experience level, how your case will be handled… and most importantly

– Whether you are comfortable with your lawyer.

It's important you feel comfortable with the lawyer you choose to represent you. Even if the lawyer is highly experienced, if you are uncomfortable with them or they don't treat you with respect, then it is likely your relationship with them will not be a good one… And let's face it; these cases can take a long, long time.

We've put together a listing of questions to help you determine which lawyer is best for you.

These "7 Crucial Questions" address important points and should be asked of anyone you are considering to help you protect your rights.

1. How long have you practiced Social Security Disability law? How many disabled clients do you represent each year?

Experience makes a difference.

Your Social Security Disability lawyer is your advocate. He or she should be experienced in this field, and have a strong focus in disability cases.

2. How many disability cases have you handled for those with my specific disability?

Lawyers are not doctors.

Those that handle primarily Social Security disability cases may be familiar with some medical conditions, but again, we are not medical professionals.

If your lawyer is not familiar with your condition, they should be willing to learn about it.

3. As a client, what are your expectations of me?

Earlier, we mentioned the "7 Most Common Mistakes You Can Make" that could result in a denial of your claim.

We really need our clients to keep us informed about what is going on with them. For example:

- New contact information or change of address
- Significant medical developments, new tests or scans
- Brand new diagnosis
- If you receive anything from the SSA, especially a decision

Also, think about asking your attorney what office practices or technology the firm has to track your case.

4. Who in your office (attorneys and other staff) will handle my disability case? What experience do these individuals have?

If the lawyer has the experience with disability cases and knowledge you want, you can bet that he or she is in court often and won't always be available at the office.

Most Social Security lawyers will use highly-trained paralegals as case managers to help you in their absence and handle client communication and record development. Find out whom in the office will be handling your issues, should the attorney not be immediately available.

5. Tell me about your client services policies.

You will want to find out what policies are in place to protect you as a client.

Keeping you informed and educated as a client, professional and ethical conduct, and client privacy protection are examples of client services you want from your lawyer.

In the event you are dissatisfied with your lawyer you will want to know who to talk to in the firm.

In our experience, the most common complaint is the time frame for these cases. Unfortunately, there is little we can do when we wait (and wait) for SS to act. The point is, make sure you have a good point of contact to go over your concerns, and see if you can get them resolved to your satisfaction.

6. How will you keep me updated on the status of my case?

During your case you'll want to know what is going on at the different levels of adjudication.

Will your law firm call you with updates or copy you on correspondence concerning your case? Now is the time to find out how informed of a client you will be. Learn when the attorney's office will call, and when you should call your attorney.

7. If I call your office, will someone be available to talk to me?

Most legal offices have junior partners or paralegals that are knowledgeable and can assist you with your case should your attorney be unavailable. (As a side note, please do not expect the receptionist to be able to handle legal questions.)

Chapter 11

A Final Note:
Protecting Your Rights Is Surprisingly Affordable. Getting Your Benefits and Providing for Your Family is *Priceless*!

Many of our clients tell us that after hiring our firm the results they see cannot be measured in dollars… This simple decision to finally have someone working on your side to protect your rights and fight for your benefits can create a number of significant positive changes.

The question is, "What is it worth to get professional help, and make sure you get the benefits you need and deserve?"

Imagine having an advocate at your side that has helped thousands of people, working diligently to protect your rights, making sure you don't get taken advantage of, taking some of the stress and pressure away... And instead, you can focus on getting better and getting your life back...

We know you would never "price shop" anything this important. However, you'll be happy to know that hiring a Social Security Disability lawyer is more affordable than you might think — and since we work on a 25% contingency fee, that means you only pay if we are able to collect for you. (You can call us at our office and we will explain all the fees fully.) Attorney fees are contingent upon winning, and they must be approved by the SSA.

You've been worrying about this for a while...

Now's your chance to consult with an experienced Social Security lawyer—and you can do so with No Charge and No Obligation what-so-ever. Also, you'll enjoy complete privacy and confidentiality.

Because we understand how important this is to you...

We just want every person who has ever been sick, injured, or disabled, and felt confused and lost about his or her situation to get the facts first, then decide if hiring a Social Security Disability attorney is right for them... without feeling pressure and financial obligation.

We know what a positive, life-long impact getting your benefits can have on you... Without having to worry about bills and expenses... fighting to get past the "I can barely survive" stage. Over our 20+ years of handling SSD cases like

47

yours, we've seen the financial devastation of being unable to work. But, it's still a big decision... and yours alone to make.

However - we suggest that you only make these kinds of decisions after a consultation with an experienced attorney, one who has a strong focus in Social Security Disability law, SSA claims procedure, and one that has a knowledgeable staff. And, we want to help you by making the decision an easy one.

So, what next?

Make the call, mention this book, and let us answer your questions. Or if you'd rather, feel free to email us personally at **whit@whitleylawfirm.com** and mention this book, and ask your questions. We never charge just to talk to you, and there is absolutely NO FEE OR ANY CHARGE unless we mutually decide to go forward and execute a written employment contract.

Please call our office at **1-800-863-1400**, between the hours of 8:00 am and 5:00 pm, Monday through Friday. Just mention this book and we will be happy to answer your questions.

We feel you are important, and not just another appointment to us. So, please be sure to bring all of your supporting documents, including any doctor reports, and prescriptions for any medications the doctors have put you on.

We are dedicated to protecting your rights and getting you the benefits you deserve—in a comfortable, professional legal setting. Here's to ending your Social Security Disability red tape and confusion!

Sincerely,

Whit Whitley and Tiana Hinnant

Appendix: Glossary of Common and Confusing Social Security Disability Terms

By now you should have a pretty good grasp on what Social Security Disability Insurance is, the protection it provides and how to file your claim.

To help you through the process, you should have a basic understanding of certain terms that will be frequently used during your claim. Here is a simplified, plain-English description of key words you may hear a lot, once your claim is filed:

Acceptable Medical Sources– To be considered as proof of your disability, your primary medical documentation and records should come from the treating physicians, hospital, rehabilitation center, laboratories, etc.

Administrative Law Judge (ALJ)– This is the judge who presides over a Disability Hearing, should your initial application and Request for Reconsideration be denied.

Appeal– A claimant (the person filing for Disability) always has the right to appeal (or try to change), the decision of the Social Security Administration when they have made a decision that affects your benefits.

Beneficiary– Anyone who receives Social Security benefits.

Benefits– Retirement, Disability, Dependents, Survivors and Medicare are the 5 categories within the Social Security system under which you may receive benefits.

Blue Book– Another name for the SSA's listings of disabling medical conditions. There are two versions – one covers adult conditions and the other lists conditions that impact children.

Child– May include your biological children or any other child who can inherit your personal property under state law, or who meets certain specific requirements under the Social Security Act.

Claimant– The person filing for Social Security benefits.

Consultative Examination– If there are questions about your medical records, the SSA may require you to submit to a medical examination by a physician of their choosing, that they pay. This doctor will not provide treatment. He or she will only examine you and send SS a written report. Failure to summit to the exam can result in a denial of your claim.

Direct Deposit– The standard way to receive Social Security benefits, they are deposited directly into your bank account.

Disability– A physical or mental condition that limits an individual's ability to work, perform or enjoy everyday activities. The SSA does not consider an individual to be "disabled" unless the condition is expected to last for more than 12 months or is expected to be terminal.

Disability Benefits– These benefits are received if the Claimant is: under full retirement age, has enough Social Security credits, and has a severe medical impairment that prevents him or her from doing substantial work for more than a year, or if he or she is expected to die from the impairment.

Disability Determination Services (DDS)– A medical review board in each state that makes the decision on whether or not an individual is disabled or behalf of the SSA.

Disabling Condition– Any medical condition that results in disability.

Earnings Record– A chronological history of the amount earned each year during a working lifetime. The credits earned remain on Social Security records even when a person

50

changes jobs or has no earnings.

Family Benefits– The following people may be eligible to receive benefits on a Claimant's record:

- Spouse, if aged 62 or older (unless caring for an entitled child under the age of 16)
- Children, if unmarried and under the age of 18 (or under 19 and still in school)
- Disabled children over the age of 18
- An ex-spouse (in some circumstances)

Family Maximum– The maximum amount of benefits payable to an entire family on any one worker's record.

Grids (also called Medical-Vocational Guidelines)– When a disability is not severe enough to generate automatic approval under the Social Security Listing, the Grids (Medical-Vocational Guidelines) are used by the SSA to help determine whether an individual should be considered disabled. Age, education and skills considered.

Impairment– The overall effect of the illness, disease or condition on the individual's ability to function. Impairment may be total or part.

Listings– Medical lists of conditions the SSA considers to be disabling. (Also called The Blue Book)

Lump Sum Death Payment– A one-time payment of $255 paid in addition to any monthly survivors' insurance benefits that are due. This benefit is paid to widows/widowers or minor children.

Maximum Earnings– The maximum earnings counted for any calendar year when computing Social Security benefits.

Representative Payee– If an individual receives Social Security benefits or Supplemental Security Income and becomes unable to handle his or her own financial affairs,

51

then a relative, friend, or an interested party is appointed to handle all Social Security matters.

Residual Functional Capacity (RFC)– An evaluation of the work skills the Claimant is still able to do, even with severe impairments.

Retroactive Benefits (Back Pay)– Monthly benefits that a Claimant may be entitled to before the month the application is actually filed if he or she meets the entitlement requirements.

Social Security– While we work, we pay taxes into the Social Security system. When we retire or become disabled, we, our spouse, and dependent children will receive monthly benefits based on our reported earnings. The system also allows survivors to collect benefits if we die.

Supplemental Security Income (SSI)– A Federal supplemental income program which helps the aging, blind, and disabled, who have little or no income, this benefit is not based upon what you paid into the SS system and is available for people who may never have worked or who stopped working years ago.

Survivor Benefits– If a Claimant dies, benefits may be paid to:
- The Claimant's spouse age 60 or older (50 or older if a disability rather than death occurs) or at any age if the spouse is caring for a child under the age of 16.
- Children age 18 or younger (19 or younger if still in school)
- Parents, if Claimant provided at least half of their financial support.

Title 2: The Social Security Disability Insurance claim is sometimes called a Title 2 claim.

Title 16: The Supplement Security Income claim is

sometimes called a Title 16 claim.

Wage Earner– A person who earns Social Security credits while working for wages or self-employment income.

Wages– All payment for services performed for an employer. If you have been compensated in ways other than cash, the cash value of that compensation is also considered wages (unless the form of payment is specifically not covered under the Social Security Act).